John Nash

'The delighted eye

John Nash. Pencil Drawing by Gilbert Spencer 1964

John Nash

'The delighted eye'

Allen Freer

SCOLAR PRESS

Published by
SCOLAR PRESS
Gower House
Croft Road
Aldershot
Hants GU11 3HR
England

Ashgate Publishing Company
Old Post Road
Brookfield
Vermont 05036
USA

British Library Cataloguing in Publication Data

Freer, Allen
  John Nash: Delighted Eye
  I. Title
  759.2

Library of Congress Cataloging-in-Publication Data

Freer, Allen.
    John Nash : the delighted eye / Allen Freer.
      p. cm.
    ISBN 0-85967-958-6
    1. Nash, John, 1893-1977—Themes, motives. I. Title.
  N6797.N36F74 1993
    759.2—dc20   93-20636
                   CIP

ISBN 0 85967 958 6 (Hbk)
ISBN 1 85928 000 5 (Pbk)

Typeset in 11 point Plantin by JL & GA Wheatley Design, Aldershot and printed in Great Britain at the University Press, Cambridge.

For all things the delighted eye now sees
Were loved by him: the old storm-broken trees
That cast their shadows upon road and bridge;
The tower set on the stream's edge;
The ford where drinking cattle made a stir
Nightly, and startled by that sound
The waterhen must change her ground;
He might have been your heartiest welcomer.

In memory of Major Robert Gregory.
W.B. Yeats

For Catharine and Mary

Contents

Preface

Throughout his life – and especially the latter end of it – John Nash always hoped that someone would make a book of his drawings and paintings. In the 1920s, The Fleuron had published a tiny book about his work with an introductory brief essay by his friend, Sidney Schiff. Sir John Rothenstein for many years intended to write about his work; but unfortunately this project was delayed until well after John Nash died in 1977. However, a year after John Nash's death, his friend and literary executor, John Lewis, compiled an excellent account of John Nash's illustrative work in 'John Nash: the painter as illustrator', distinguished by its judicious selection of material and the care and beauty of its presentation. This was followed by Jeremy Greenwood's thorough and masterly account of John Nash's wood-engravings and lithographs. Clare Colvin's catalogue for The Minories Exhibition in 1985 completed the work on the book illustrations with scholarly and sensitive insight. And Sir John Rothenstein brought out his biography of the painter in 1983, six years after the painter's death.

The present work seeks to complement the work of the foregoing writers in that it concentrates wholly on John Nash's oil paintings and drawings, in watercolours, pencil and ink. The selection is as representative as it was possible to make it. Many of the items in this selection have never been reproduced before. It is hoped that they will not only give pleasure to those who are already admirers of John Nash's achievement but that, in addition, they will afford an interesting introduction to those not already familiar with his work.

In all this, I have been both encouraged and helped by many private collectors and friends of the artist who have delighted in his work for many years. My sincere thanks are due to them all: that they are not named specifically is one more sign of our less than honest times.

I must, however, thank Ronald Blythe who has encouraged me from the outset. Over the years he has most generously shared with me his insights into John Nash's personality and his ways of work. I would also like to thank John Lewis for his immediate help and encouragement. David Wolfers, John Nash's artistic executor has given me the benefit of his extensive knowledge of John Nash's painting for which

I am most grateful. My thanks, too, for the help accorded me by Robin Vousden of the Anthony d'Offay Gallery and Anthony Spink and Edward King of Spink and Son. To Richard Littlewood, Douglas Attfield, Adrian Pope and Michael Dudley my thanks for their photographs and their care and co-operation in their various assignments. Also, I would thank all those directors and keepers in both national and provincial galleries who have, in an increasingly busy life, put their knowledge and help at my disposal.

Finally, I wish to thank my wife for her help and support without which I should not have undertaken this book in the first place, nor managed to bring it to what I hope is a satisfactory conclusion.

AF

Acknowledgements

The authors and publishers would like to thank the following museums and galleries for their kind assistance in providing illustrations and giving permission for them to be reproduced:

Anthony d'Offay Gallery: 'Trees by the Sea, Norfolk', *The Artist Plantsman*

Ashmolean Museum, Oxford: 'Gloucestershire Landscape'.

Birmingham Museum and Art Gallery: 'Winter Afternoon'.

Buckinghamshire County Museum: 'The Woodland Ride', 'Whiteleaf Woods in Summer', 'Sunlight and Shadow', 'Threshing in a farmyard near Princes Risborough', 'Father Christmas Fishing', 'Carline Thistles in a jam jar'.

Chelmsford Museum Service: 'Cliffs at Covehithe', 'Wormingford Mill'.

Colchester Borough Council: 'The Garden in Winter'.

Fitzwilliam Museum, Cambridge: 'The Edge of the Plain'.

Trustees of The Imperial War Museum: 'Over the Top', 'Oppy Wood, Evening', 'A Bombing Post in the Snow'.

Ipswich Borough Council Museums and Galleries: 'Granaries, Ipswich'.

Leeds City Art Gallery: 'The Viaduct', 'Trees in a flood', 'Hillside Whiteleaf'.

Leicester Museum and Art Gallery: 'The Timber Stack, Chiltern Woods'.

The Medici Society and the Tate Gallery, London: 'The Cornfield'.

The Board of Trustees of the National Museums and Galleries in Merseyside: 'Disused Gravel Pit', 'Incoming Tide, Overstrand'.

Northampton Museums and Art Gallery: 'The Deserted Sheep-pen'.

Towner Art Gallery, Eastbourne: 'Disused Canal at Wormingford'.

Spink and Son: 'About a Pig', 'A Game of Croquet', 'Iver Heath', 'Hillside at Night', 'Interior of a Wood', 'Dunwich', 'French Landscape', 'Tuscan Landscape'.

The Whitworth Gallery, University of Manchester: 'Woods in Winter'.

Grateful acknowledgement is made to the Anthony d'Offay Gallery for permission to reprint John Nash's autobiographical essay, *The Artist Plantsman*, first published as a limited edition booklet to commemorate John Nash's exhibition of flower drawings at the d'Offay Gallery in 1976.

Chronology

1893	John Nash born April 11 at Ghuznee Lodge, Sunningdale Gardens, Earl's Court, London. His father was William Harry Nash, Recorder of Abingdon and his mother, Caroline Maude, was daughter of Captain Milbourne Jackson R.N. His elder brother, Paul, had been born in 1889.
1895	Birth of Barbara Milbourne Nash, John Nash's only sister.
1901	The family moved to Wood Lane House, Iver Heath, Buckinghamshire.
1905–1909	John Nash attended Langley Place School between Uxbridge and Slough.
1909–1911	John Nash's education continued at Wellington College. In school holidays John and his brother made frequent visits to art galleries and the Victoria and Albert Museum.
1910	Death of Caroline Maude Nash on 4th February.
1910–1911	Roger Fry's first Post-Impressionist Exhibition.
1912	Worked as a junior unpaid reporter for the Middlesex and Buckinghamshire Advertiser. The post was relinquished after a few months' work in August 1912.
1912	Critical appraisal and encouragement given to John Nash by Gordon Bottomley and Claughton Pellew-Harvey. John went on walking tours of Norfolk with Claughton Pellew who succeeded in persuading John Nash to be an artist rather than a journalist.
1912–1913	October 1912–January 1913. Second Post-Impressionist Exhibition. John Nash visited neither of these exhibitions. Became friendly with Edward Marsh.
1913	In November, the Exhibition of Drawings by Paul and John Nash at the Dorien Leigh Gallery, Pelham Street, South Kensington met with considerable success. As a consequence both brothers invited to become members of the Friday Club.
1914	John Nash elected founder member of the London Group 3rd January 1914. Exhibited at their first exhibition – 'a grand coalition of radicals' – at the

Goupil Galleries whose proprietor, William Marchant became John's dealer until his death. Mrs. Marchant continued to act as John's dealer until her death in 1958. In January 1914 John Nash visited Italy, staying at the Villa le Pergole at Careggi outside Florence.

August 4th 1914: Outbreak of First World War.

Autumn 1914: Worked as an agricultural labourer in Dorset.

October 1914: Sworn in as a Special Constable for Buckingham.

1915   Exhibited with the Cumberland Market Group with Gilman, Ginner and Bevan. Sir Michael Sadler purchased his 'Trees in a Flood' and presented it to Leeds Art Gallery. This was the first picture to be acquired for a public collection. Early in 1915 he worked at making tents for the Army.

1916   In February he took a clerical post at the Ministry of Munitions in Northumberland Avenue. In September, John Nash enlisted in the Artists' Rifles, 28th London Regiment. After preliminary training, he was sent to the Western Front where he made a bid for a commission in May 1917.

1917   In June, John Nash was given a course of training at Oppy Wood on the Belgian Front. His unit was sent to the Front Line in the same month.

July 1917. John Nash much frustrated by his failure to obtain a commission. In November 1917 Paul met him at the Front 'a bronzed and tattered soldier with incredible hands overgrown with cuticle'.

Action on December 30th 1917 (commemorated subsequently in 'Over the Top', his most notable war painting). The action 'was pure murder and I was lucky to escape untouched'.

1918   Late in January 1918 he came home on leave and was officially demobilised in February in order to become an official War Artist. On 13th May, John Nash was commissioned as an honorary Second Lieutenant in the 2nd Battalion of the Artists' Rifles. This enabled him to draw Army pay and to be provided with a uniform so that he could revisit the Western Front should he need to do so. In May married to Christine Külenthal, daughter of Wilhelm Heinrich Külenthal and Ada Josephine Bustin. Gilbert Spencer was the best man.

June: Started to work on 'Oppy Wood', his first major war painting. The painting was carried out in a former herb-drying shed in Chalfont St. Peter near Gerrards Cross. The shed was shared by his brother Paul as a studio.

Autumn: 'The Cornfield' painted.

1919   Left Chalfont St. Peter and took a flat above a chemist's shop in Gerrards Cross. The summer was spent at Whiteleaf near Princes Risborough.

1921   First one-man exhibition at Goupil Gallery which proved to be very successful. Became an early member of the Society of Wood Engravers.

1922   Left Gerrards Cross in the Spring to live in Lane End House, Meadle, near Aylesbury.

1924–
1929 Taught at the Ruskin School of Art in Oxford.

1927 Publication of *Poisonous Plants: Deadly, Dangerous and Suspect*: one of the most distinguished of the Haslewood Press books published by Frederick Etchells and Hugh MacDonald. Wood engravings and introduction by John Nash.

1930 Second one-man show at Goupil Galleries.
Birth of his son William.
Publication of *The Shepheards Calendar* by Edmund Spenser, Cresset Press. Hand-coloured line illustrations by John Nash.

1933 Exhibition at the French Gallery.

1934–
1940 Taught in the Design School of the Royal College of Art, London where apart from the war years he remained until 1957.

1935 Death of his son William.
Publication of *Flowers and Faces* by H.E. Bates with wood engravings by John Nash. Published by the Golden Cockerel Press.

1937 *Bucks Shell Guide* by John Nash with notes on the monuments by Katherine A. Esdaile. Published by Batsford.
Executed large design for the Paris Exhibition.

1939 First visit to the Gower Peninsula, Glamorgan to which he returned on several occasions.
Outbreak of the Second World War, Sept 3rd.

1940 Appointed Official War Artist to the Admiralty.
Served in Plymouth, Swansea and Bristol.
Elected Associate of the Royal Academy.
Applied for transfer to Active Service.

1941 In March he was commissioned as Captain, later Acting Major in the Royal Marines on the staff of the C in C in Rosyth and Portsmouth.

1943 Bottemgoms Farm, Wormingford, Essex purchased for £750.

1944 John Nash discharged from the Forces. Lane End House, Meadle sold by the Nashes who moved into Bottemgoms Farm.

1946 Death of his brother, Paul Nash.

1948 *English Garden Flowers* published by Duckworth.

1951 John Nash elected Royal Academician.

1954 Retrospective exhibition at the Leicester Galleries, London.

1957 First of regular visits to Skye.

1958 John Nash began regular annual botanical illustration classes at the Flatford Mill Field Studies Centre.

1964 Awarded C.B.E.

1967 Major retrospective exhibition 'John Nash C.B.E., R.A.', at the Royal Academy.

Awarded an honorary degree by the University of Essex.

1972   *The Natural History of Selborne* by Gilbert White with an introduction by the Earl of Cranbrook published by the Limited Editions Club with John Nash's illustrations.

1976   Exhibition at Anthony d'Offay Gallery of 'Plants and Flowers'. *The Artist Plantsman* published by Anthony d'Offay for the exhibition.
Death of Christine Nash.

1977   Death of John Nash 23rd September 1977.

Principal exhibitions

1913   Dorien Leigh Gallery, London – with Paul Nash.
16 December 1913 – 19 January 1914: Brighton Public Art Gallery – 'The Camden Town Group, Vorticists & Others'.

1915   Goupil Gallery, London – with the Cumberland Market Group (Robert Bevan, Harold Gilman, and Charles Ginner).

1921   Goupil Gallery, London – first one-man show.

1930   Goupil Gallery, London.

1933   The French Gallery, London.

1938   Little Burlington Gallery, London.

1939   Goupil Gallery, London.

1950   Harris Museum & Art Gallery, Preston.

1953   Aldeburgh Festival, Suffolk.
Graves Art Gallery, Sheffield.

1954   Leicester Galleries, London – retrospective.

1960   Leicester Galleries, London.

1967   Royal Academy of Arts, London – 'John Nash CBE RA'.
The Minories, Colchester.

1970   Hamet Gallery, London.

1971   Worthing Art Gallery.

1973   Anthony d'Offay Gallery, London.

1974   Maltzahn Gallery, London.

1976   Anthony d'Offay Gallery – 'The Artist Plantsman'.

1978   Blond Fine Art, London – 'Paul Nash and John Nash'.

1980   Aldeburgh Festival, Suffolk.

Marrow and Sunflower

Introduction

Before it was blown down in the great gale which swept ruthlessly over southern England and Suffolk in the mid eighties, the black barn was the building where you left the country road and took to the field track which soon dipped with the curve of the land. As the track sloped and rose, so the hedges on either side of it closed their hazels over it, making in summer a green tunnel at the end of which was the light and the open field and the road slanting gently into the valley until it petered out at a notice: 'Cars Turn Here'. Though they could barely be seen in summer because of the high gunneras and bamboos surrounding them, here were two ponds and also an old wooden garage rendered inconspicuous by stems and leaves. The field track now became a mown path leading through an orchard of old apple and plum trees to the flagged path – stepping stones through the magical garden which always seemed about to engulf benignly in its green tide of growth the old farm house – Bottemgoms Farm. Beyond the house and garden were more clustered trees through which one glimpsed the fields that undulated down the Valley of the Stour. To come upon this place at any time of year was a wonder, astringent yet strangely welcoming in winter, burgeoning and voluptuous in high summer. It was like being able to walk into a pastoral dream, at once commonplace, rural, workaday and yet, extraordinary. Here John Nash and his wife Christine lived for the last thirty or so years of their lives. No other place could be more appropriate for a man who knew himself to be a countryman, an artist and a plantsman.

Yet his beginnings were a world away from this, for he was born in London on 11 April 1893, the second of three children born to Caroline Maude and William Harry Nash. His elder brother, Paul, had been born four years before, his sister Barbara was born two years later. William Harry Nash was a barrister-at-law who later became Recorder of Abingdon; his wife's family had naval connections. There was no artistic tradition in the family and the only family link with the world of painting came through his Aunt Gussie's friendship with Edward Lear.

John's first eight years were spent in Kensington. Their home, the strangely named Ghuznee Lodge we always see through Paul's eyes, '... not an attractive house and I never loved it ... a pariah of a house with its outlandish name and its pretentious conservatory where nothing, *ever*, would grow. Certainly it did not belong where it was.' He writes of 'the dining room which lived in a sort of warm gloom' and 'the drawing room an entirely unreal place to me, which led, quite logically, to the mocking glass void with its withered plants.'

How objective this account is we shall never really know. What it points to is an almost overwhelming sense of place: and an awareness of a sense of place is a characteristic shared acutely by both brothers. Even so, Paul's account does seem to point to a feeling of malaise that settled on the house owing to family circumstances. For it was an ill-at-ease family owing to Mrs. Nash's condition. We know little more than that she was delicate, an invalid, prone to moodiness and depression; a condition which became more frequent and intense with the passage of time. It was as much an urgent need to alleviate her condition as an instinctual longing to return to the countryside of his forbears that led William Harry to acquire an acre and a half of land at Iver Heath in what was then rural Buckinghamshire, 'leafy Bucks', the county in which Nashes had farmed for centuries. It was for Paul 'real country' they were to live in, when they went to live in Wood Lane House in 1902, and yet it was no more than fifteen miles from the centre of London and the Inns of Court.

Despite the move, Mrs. Nash's condition became worse and steadily deteriorated over the next eight years and she spent increasingly longer periods under medical care in nursing homes and asylums until her death in 1910. Though relatives rallied in support for and help to the family, the children were thrown back on themselves, the father increasingly dependent on Paul, John and his sister in a close alliance with each other. However, the move to Iver Heath proved beneficial to the children in this respect: it was here that their education began, if by education we mean that 'very culture of the feelings' that would shape and determine their lives. It was here they had a chance to become what they, in their blood, always felt themselves to be: countrymen, in the country, alive to the changing seasons and to the life, growth and decay of the trees and plants around them. The natives had returned indeed!

John Nash lived in Buckinghamshire for thirty-eight years. There were absences – his two years at Wellington College; his service in France during the First World War, various painting expeditions, forays for landscapes – but it was in this county that he had his roots; its landscapes stimulated the artist and played no small part in conditioning his sensibility. From the outset at Iver Heath he discovered his delight in gardening, even if his efforts there met with scant success. Thirty or so years after he came to Buckinghamshire his intimate knowledge of its hills, woods, towns and villages led to his writing, with a delicacy of wit and insight, the first *Shell Guide to Buckinghamshire* which was published in 1937.

But this is to anticipate. After being educated by governesses at home, he attended Langley Place School from 1905 to 1909 and then went, with an uncle's financial help, to Wellington College for the next two years. Life at an Edwardian Public School with its compulsory games and rigorous routines was scarcely a place to guarantee the happiness of a sensitive boy. Fortunately, he had enough 'nous' to see that by choosing to play Fives he could avoid compulsory cricket and secure sufficient time to ramble off and collect specimens of plants and flowers. Here are the beginnings of considerable botanical knowledge which is personal and specific. He was always proud of the fact that he won the Botany Prize at the end of his two years at Wellington: it confirmed his interest. But the interest would be sustained throughout his life because the roots of it went very deep. He was a gardener – a plantsman, to use his own term – by instinct.

What he was to do when he left Wellington was clear to none of the family, nor to himself. In this, he was no different from many seventeen year olds: no clear idea of his vocation, vague aspirations of what he might do, limited financial resources (Mrs. Nash's medical bills had certainly strained his father's finances). His brother Paul tells us that various professions were considered: 'The Church, a diplomatic career, journalism' and concedes that these were 'the wildest schemes' though he adds that John had 'the mentality of a scholar' but then qualifies this by saying that 'as yet it was no more than an attitude' and later speaks of his 'fine dark profile and his scholarly, slightly elaborate manner of talking'. Even before the First World War it would surely have required more qualities than these to get him into Oxford where, the family thought, he might go. Being 'a man of letters' required more than the right appearance and manner.

The fact that he failed to secure a place at Oxford and that his father was unable to finance his entry into the legal profession led him to take a practical step towards becoming a writer. In the summer of 1912 he served for a few months as a cub reporter for the *Middlesex and Buckinghamshire Advertiser*. The work for the paper absorbed both time and energy. In pursuit of copy he had to ride 'on his bicycle all over the county at all hours of the day and night' – and this, at least, served a deeper purpose as he acquired a first-hand knowledge of Buckinghamshire in all its variety. There is, after all, no better way of getting the very feel of an area than by walking over it or cycling through it both in the light and in the darkness.

In what time he had at his disposal he had also started to make drawings – comic drawings and, now and again, landscapes: the first for fun, the latter were his first attempts to come to grips with the lie of the land. Was his choice of the subject, one wonders, conditioned not only by what he saw Paul doing, but more potently, a recollection of what he had seen in something like abundance at his Aunt Gussie's? She, who had known Edward Lear so well and been adored by him – (though he could never bring himself to propose to her as he considered himself ludicrously ugly and an epileptic to boot) – had been the recipient of many of Lear's landscape watercolours. It was she who introduced the Nash children to the Nonsense rhymes and Stories and gave them coloured copies 'no doubt first editions'. No one can encounter Lear's drawings and verses and forget them; they become one's nonsense for ever, and the Nash children never did forget her soft voice reading in slightly exaggerated tones: 'There was an old man with a beard'.

It is unlikely that the Lear watercolours made less effect. Paul speaks of them as 'dry, luminous .... the first watercolours that I had seen' and continues 'he [Lear] got carried away into surprising beauties of landscape painting and his drawings seldom lacked structure'. One wonders more and more how deep the impression was on John. Certainly his painting and his drawing have readily discernable affinities with the work of Lear which he saw as a small boy on his visits to his Aunt Gussie's drawing room in Elm Park Gardens. Recollections of Lear's work provided, albeit tentatively and subtly, a kind of model of what an artist might legitimately engage with: comedy – even farce – and landscape.

However conjectural this may be, John tended to be diffident about his drawing, though he must have had sufficient confidence to show some of his work to the editor of the *Middlesex and Buckinghamshire Advertiser* who decided to publish one of the drawings in the paper. It was the first 'John Nash' to appear in print: a brief moment of recognition. Who, seeing it, could imagine the vast amount of illustrative work John was to accomplish in the next sixty years? Very few, least of all the artist himself.

Yet help was at hand in the form of encouragement and a firm belief in his ability and worth. Three men, each in his own way, gave John that true and fructifying support that was most necessary to him at this very early stage of his development. Through their belief in his vision, ability and artist's nature, they played an enormously important part in his career. 'You have to be strong to be an artist', Winifred Nicholson once said. And those who support a beginning artist need strength too, strength of discernment and perception and an overwhelming feeling that the young and untried artist has the heart of the matter in him. The three men were his brother Paul, Gordon Bottomley and Claughton Pellew-Harvey, a friend of Paul's at the Slade. Of these three, Paul played the most important role in encouraging and fostering John's nascent talent as his letters written in 1912 and 1913 to Gordon Bottomley show. Bottomley, a poet and playwright as well as a collector of discernment, had given Paul much enthusiastic encouragement after he had seen Paul's drawings to accompany his verse-drama 'The Crier by Night'. A correspondence began between the two men which was to last the whole of Paul's lifetime. But it is the early stages of this correspondence which are of specific interest. They show Bottomley to have been unusually sensitive, and aware of the ability and the vision of both Paul and John Nash. Paul would send Bottomley packets of his own drawings and paintings for comment. They would be returned with suggestions and criticism. As Bottomley had been so helpful over his work, Paul decided to send him several items by John. He needed to be reassured by Bottomley that what he had seen and admired in his brother's work was something authentic and distinctive. He needed to risk not only his brother's work but also his own judgement. If John's work had the interest and approval of his own mentor, then the encouragement that he (Paul) had given John was far from misplaced.

At the end of May 1912, Paul wrote to Bottomley:

Instead I venture to try and amuse you by sending you some of the drawings of John N. Nash brother of Paul. These start for the North tomorrow (if Jack will let them) with the hope you will see the fun of them. *To me they are great and like no-one else's.*

There was some slight delay in replying, since the Bottomleys had left Cartmel for a recuperative stay in Buxton. But in early July, Bottomley returned the drawings and wrote to Paul about them:

We enjoyed your brother's drawings greatly (being particularly impressed by his profound belief that the human countenance fundamentally resembles a bird's), and we were constantly finding touches and passages to admire. We think he shows real promise – considerable promise. I don't know how the instinct of draughtsmanship entered your family, but it is there and it could be useless to try to chill it. He has not only a good sense of the decorative disposition of his masses, but his blacks have a beautiful quality, and his pen-touch is crisp and clear and delicate and exquisitely balanced. You do not say what your father is thinking of making of him; but in any case these are qualities of tact as valuable in human conduct as they are in art, and it can do him nothing but good to give rein to his feeling for drawing. In facility and lucidity and directness of expression, and in his faculty of keeping his material untroubled, he has advantages over you; but of course it remains to be seen if he can pursue these qualities when he has as much to say as you have. His fun is first-rate, we adored the foot-and-mouth asylum hugely. In another way we thought his railway nocturnes full of good qualities and of feeling for beautiful night. In still another way we found his Madame Mysterieuse interesting; for if he has never seen work by Conder or Gordon Craig he has made in it quite remarkable discoveries about the handling and quality of water colour.

Not surprisingly, this detailed response, manifesting as it does a delicate but real perceptiveness of the potential of the submitted work, received a delighted reply:–

I was right glad to have your splendid letter you have a seemingly inexhaustible store of generous words. Jack is very much 'set up for the rest of 'is natural', as the vulgar have it, upon your high praise – I do not mean he has swollen his headpiece for he ever expresses a mild surprise at any appreciation upon his drawings, which he does at odd times on odd pieces of paper when he has nothing else to do. I, from time to time, raid his desk or the waste paper basket or the corners of the room and collect the odd bits of paper like a park-keeper in Kensington Gardens, and after a sorting of chaff from grain tho to be sure it is all 'chaff' I select the best and cut them into a decent shape and mount them. At first Jack used to be so delighted at the good appearance of his drawings when mounted that he fully believed it was entirely owing to the way I set them up and drew lines round them; gradually it has dawned on him that it must be that he has done a good drawing – this is a pity because he has now become a little too conscious and careful, with the result his designs are not so naive and simple. At present he is working on the staff of a country paper and gaining experience for a journalistic career. All his abilities lie in that direction and he will tell you that his ambition is to be 'a man of letters'. These drawings are as yet his only expression of himself. He is very observant and writes excellent descriptions of things that strike him, always with the same quaint touch you see in these designs.

Paul was nothing if not a great encourager of his brother's drawing and painting. He saw at once that John's art had a quality, naïve, and direct, even innovatory that set it apart from his own work and the work he saw his fellow students producing under the critical eye of Henry Tonks and Fred Brown at the Slade. To be sure, work was being done at the Slade of very considerable distinction: but it did not have this special quality that John's had. He had a kind of innocent eye that would be ruined in next to no time were it to submit to the strictures of the Slade teachers. John's gift was rather like a state of grace which certain chosen people are endowed with. It could not be had by wishing or working for it and, like innocence, could easily be corrupted or even destroyed. Bottomley had also identified the distinction and personal vision in John's drawings so that his detailed analysis and comment ratified Paul's judgement and justified his encouragement which was steadily pushing John in the direction of a painter's career by the week.

It was, however, another friend of Paul's who finally set the seal on John's decision to be an artist. This was Claughton Pellew-Harvey, a fellow-student at the Slade whom Paul found to be especially congenial. He admired Paul's work, discussed art and life with him, invited Paul to stay at the family home in Blackheath and was invited back to the Nash home at Iver Heath, thus encountering John and Barbara. This 'slight dark man with a strange voice which was oddly attractive and his profound magnetic eyes, capable of laughing' had no small effect on the Nash family. He simply was the sort of person difficult to define but hard to forget. Paul went on a walking holiday with him in Norfolk for these were the days of the Open Road. George Borrow was a potent influence and 'Lavengro', with its wanderings and encounters spoke a language and evoked a world of gypsy freedom and liberated escape. From this holiday in Norfolk Paul produced one of the most strange and striking pictures amongst his early work, the 'Cliff to the North'. When a second walking holiday was to have taken place, Paul was unable to go and John went instead and came back to Iver now fully resolved to be an artist. 'Then you had better do it here,' said his father, clearing a space for him on the family dining-room table.

It would be hard to identify specifically how and why Claughton Pellew had such a decisive effect on John's scarcely declared intention to be an artist. After all, he had had no training, whereas Paul and Claughton Pellew were both being properly trained at the Slade. He was naturally diffident. Yet he had a small body of work which showed not only to his brother, but to his brother's strange but thoughtful and perceptive friend that there was a gift here, a quality that must be maintained and fostered. Paul said that it was 'Pellew who had done so much to help me in my first stages [who] seemed to be able to get Jack going in earnest'. Years later, in 1967, after Claughton Pellew's death, John wrote in a letter to his niece:

> In the beginning of my so-called career I derived so much help and inspiration from him that I can never forget it and am always grateful. He must also have greatly influenced my brother when they first met at the Slade. Alas he seemed fated to work for and help others and denied himself the full exercise of his own talents. Poor dear man he was the most unselfish of beings.

The help and inspiration came in the first place from Pellew's vision. 'He had a deep love for the country, particularly for certain of its features, such as ricks and stooks of corn. At first I was unable to understand an almost devotional approach to a haystack and listened doubtfully to a rhapsody on its beauty of form. Slowly, however, the individual beauty of certain things, trees particularly, began to dawn upon me.' Thus, Paul and John shared in the same way of looking. It was to dominate John's attitude to landscape for the rest of his life. This 'looking at' with intensity, then noting down in sketchbooks for later use in the studio so that the recollection of the thing seen should not slip into a facile generalisation, was a habit cultivated and developed. And Pellew also helped him to look meaningfully at landscape, to come to grips with the lie of the land and to feel for its spaces and enclosures and the significance of the 'placings' of hedges, ditches and trees.

Paul had already shown twenty of his drawings at the Carfax Gallery in October 1912. It was now important for both brothers to hold a joint exhibition as soon as they had sufficient work of quality to exhibit. This they did in November 1913 at the Dorien-Leigh Gallery – not really a gallery but a shop, run by two men who designed and made lampshades. Though this made it scarcely prestigious, in the event it served its purpose admirably. It cost only £2/10/- per week to rent it; and, urged by William Rothenstein (a great admirer of Paul's work) in the first instance, it was well-patronised by those concerned with artists of promise. Twenty-five paintings were exhibited and half or more were sold: even at an early stage, seven of John's and five of Paul's. Paul sent off an elated letter to Gordon Bottomley: 'The show is a success beyond our highest hopes'. It was a success not only in the sale of pictures but because those who came and bought them were distinguished and important collectors like Michael Sadler and Charles Rutherston. Apart from sales, the exhibition aroused a great deal of interest and acclaim. Here were two young English artists who were actually Post-Impressionists, innovators by instinct, whose work was above the usual rut of English landscape painting. To be both English and Modern was no small achievement in 1913. The general verdict of the most informed visitors was the same as Sir William Richmond's when first shown some of Paul's drawings, 'These are something new'. Even Roger Fry was impressed!

On the strength of their achievement both brothers were invited to show with the Camden Town Group in their Brighton exhibition a week after the Dorien-Leigh show and both were invited to become members of the Friday Club whose members were: Albert Rutherston, Mark Gertler, Roger Fry, Duncan Grant, Vanessa Bell and C.R.W. Nevinson. One has 'arrived' when there is general acclamation of one's contemporaries and peers. No greater acknowledgement could be wished. With confidence and buoyancy Paul could write to Gordon Bottomley and tell him in this first flush of success: 'We are quite the rising young men'. They also became members of the London Group whose exhibitions were first held in March 1914. Harold Gilman was the President and it was he who helped and advised John with his work in oils – a new medium for him and one in which he felt John surpassed his brother. It was Gilman who taught John to use paint unmixed with oil, and opaque rather than transparent colours. He also advised him to paint from drawings, never on the spot. The drawings (or watercolours) should be made *en plein air* but were to be squared up and worked from in the studio. It appears to be unexceptionable advice and on the whole quite sound and systematic. One wonders if its effects were always satisfactory in so far as by the time the artist arrives at his canvas, the immediacy, the first impact, has been worked over several times and there is a manifest lack of spontaneity and freshness. The water colour stage of a John Nash painting is often the most successful. It has a bloom and vitality missing in the more ponderous and substantial oil. This is not to deny the extraordinary achievement of John Nash's best work in oils which is, by common consent, memorable. But John Nash was aware of it himself. He knew that, by and large, his best work was in watercolours. This was the medium that suited his particular gifts. Line could work with colour far more easily in watercolour and he could control tone and form with an easier grace than was possible in the denser medium. Nevertheless it has to be admitted that in these early oil paintings his work can be favourably compared with his brother's. The spatial relationships, the air, the light, not only that descending in a sunburst, but that which plays around and gives solidity to the trees and cornstooks in 'Gloucestershire Landscape' (1913) vouch for the sureness of touch and the clarity of the artist's vision. It is a remarkable painting by a young man of twenty.

What never ceases to amaze is John Nash's rapid development as an artist in the years between 1912 and 1915. At the beginning of 1912 he had very little to show: what he had to hand was minimal. Yet within three years his vision and technique had matured at an almost unpredictable rate – even if one takes into consideration the fact that John was a most systematic worker. Throughout the whole of his life he worked steadily and methodically each day. He never was erratic in his ways and thus never waited for the moment of inspiration suddenly to descend. His application was consistently maintained and this guaranteed that his natural gifts could be strengthened with practice and use. The development is most strikingly seen in his landscapes which are notable for the intensity of vision communicated with an edgy directness which springs from those naïve qualities, identified earlier by his brother, working with a technical assurance of quite a different order. One has but to compare the rather austere and awkward drawings that he made in Norfolk in the area around Sheringham and Mundesley-on-Sea after visits to Norfolk with Claughton Pellew with his drawing of the Misbourne Valley in Buckinghamshire or compare both these drawings with the landscape of the Meon Valley where the richness of colour and the handling of the forms have a sophistication indicative of his growth in technique as well as in feeling. The Meon Valley painting is distinguished. Who else at that time would have used that haunting cerulean blue for the trees to offset the green of the mounds, or the one dark tree on the right of picture, painted in a blackish green so that it forms a point of meaningful emphasis? Structurally too, the painting is significant. The eye is led by stealth into the depths of the picture by a series of subtly placed screens of colour that diminish as they reach the horizon, pitched high in the picture; and their pattern is re-echoed by a series of dark broadening bands of cirrus cloud in the yellowing sky. The effect is both 'flat' and yet magically recessive. It is a picture one feels one could travel into. And yet more impressive than the subtlety of structure and colour is the atmosphere generated: it has a kind of spell-bound calm that is uncannily disconcerting, almost as if Time had had a stop. John Nash kept this picture by him for most of his lifetime and it is not hard to see why.

Even more accomplished is his 'Tuscan Landscape', the fruit of a brief Italian tour which he made in January 1914 on the strength of his profits from the sale of his pictures at the Dorien-Leigh Gallery and at other shows. Tuscany in January may lack the attractions it offers so amply later in the year. Although the landscape did not immediately appeal to John, ('I find it difficult to do landscapes here owing to the lack of open country. The mountains are very fine but never appear unless it is very clear') the view in winter which he painted months later distils the very essence of Tuscany, its hills and cultivated slopes and the punctuation of the cypress trees culminating in the huge tree on the left which dominates the picture, its soaring opacity contrasting with the wiry branches of the orchard trees. Colour, texture and pattern work together towards a vivid realisation of the thing not only seen but felt. The recollection of the landscape exerts its particular power on the painter – and the effect is as compelling as the advance in his technique. And his work at this time in watercolour is paralleled with his paintings in oils, few though these were. It has already been noted in 'Gloucestershire landscape'; but is matched by, some might say surpassed by, 'The Viaduct' painted in 1915/16 and exhibited in the London Group show in 1916 and also the painting 'Threshing' (1915). The modernity which so struck his contemporaries can be immediately discerned in 'The Viaduct' with its play of contrasting curves and swelling and receding forms of hillside and woods with both the train and its smoke cutting a line diagonally and dramatically across the picture. In 'Threshing' (1915), the energy of the picture seems to be gathered into the threshing machine itself; an affectionate but powerful puffing monster ministering in its clumsy and smokily efficient way to the needs of the harvest. At a time when the Futurists and Vorticists were extolling the beauty and importance of the machine, here is a picture that at once endorses a machine's power but somehow manages to humanise it. It is salutary to compare John Nash's treatment of the threshing machine with Thomas Hardy's description of it in *Tess of the D'Urbervilles*. In the novel, Tess is seen as a martyr to the monster that has invaded the age-old harvesting ritual; whereas twenty years on from the writing of 'Tess', the machine is seen as the indispensable servant of those who work with it. Its presentation, like the train on the viaduct, implies no moral protest.

Threshing machines were to be the subject of a number of paintings and some engravings that John Nash made between 1912 and the 1920s. It was the only industrial object that he painted, apart from ships. One wonders if this was as close to a mechanism as he wanted to go. On the other hand, a threshing machine was a sort of enhanced agricultural implement and as such was acceptable as a subject for his art which was centred mainly on the earth, water and plants, from the smallest daisy to the tallest tree. Yet in all these early works whatever the subject there is no hesitancy, no artistic stammering. They have a compelling conviction about them that makes them instantly 'understood'. Sir John Rothenstein once wrote that John Nash painted 'with vehemence and directness'. 'Vehemence' is a strange word to use about John Nash's paintings and drawings. But the more one sees of them the more appropriate it seems. It is not a harsh moral vehemence or an aggressive polemical technique: it has more to do with the striking quality of his artistic integrity which is vouched for by the discipline of his line and the purity of colour. Like any genuine and instinctive artist he knew he had limitations: but, these being acknowledged, he had now sufficient confidence to know how he could work to the full within these limitations so that each advance could be consolidated and developed.

Much has been said of John's lack of formal training. Indeed as he grew older he expressed regret that he had not been through the disciplines and rigours of an art school. How much professional tuition would have affected his work it is impossible to say. What can be said is that he did absorb a great deal from his brother's example, both deliberately and by daily contact. He also was well aware of the work of many of Paul's friends and was not slow to realise that if he was to be taken seriously, he must make his work, if not in any way similar to theirs, at least worthy of their interest. And it also has to be remembered that those precious creative years before the First World War were alive with eager and extraordinarily gifted artists, many of whom were Paul's friends and acquaintances. As Frederick Gore points out in his wholly admirable introduction to the catalogue of John Nash's Paintings at the Royal Academy in 1967, 'In 1913 London contained a galaxy of talented artists. Prominent among the moderns in their twenties were Roberts, Wadsworth, Grant, Gaudier-Brzeska, Etchells, Nevinson, the Spencers, the Carlines, Vanessa Bell, Boris Anrep: in their thirties, Bevan, Ginner, Gilman, Gore, Wyndham Lewis, Epstein and Gill'. It is a formidable list and even if one was only on the periphery of this world of painters one must have been aware of their potential and also of their achievement. But especially in John's case, not *too* aware, not *too* much embroiled, because by becoming too much involved there was a threat to one's artistic stance. To be at the centre of the latest and most passionately held ideas can, in the end, lead to theories that do not facilitate or simplify, but act like tripwires. John Nash was not *in* this artistic milieu but still *of* it. He was thus never isolated and so turned in on himself that his development was imperilled. This does not alter the fact that both as a young artist and subsequently throughout his life he tended to avoid talking about his art or even the art of his contemporaries. He fought shy of theories, had few books on art but many on gardening, flowers, music and fishing. Among his most prized possessions was a run of *Curtis's Botanical Magazine*, whose exquisite and accurate engravings inspired his own botanical work as much as the flowers and plants in his garden. It was the quality of his response that mattered and his art must bear witness to that response in all its particularities. But concern for the development of his art was now overshadowed by the outbreak of the First World War in August 1914.

Curiously, the war did not affect John Nash directly at first. Shortly after the war broke out he worked in Dorset as an agricultural labourer. So also did Paul. In October he was sworn in as a Special Constable for Buckingham and then moved temporarily to London to make tents for the army at Mappin and Webb. As late as February 1916, having been rejected by the army, he took a clerical post at the Ministry of Munitions in Northumberland Avenue, often staying in London with his patron and friend, Edward Marsh. In what time he had to himself he continued to paint in oils and watercolours though the opportunity to do so was limited. It was not until September 1916 that he was finally able to enlist in the Artists' Rifles, the 28th London Regiment. He served with them from November 1916 until January 1918.

Shortly before his embarkation to France he made the remarkable drawing of an uprooted tree, seen sprawled on the ground, its twigs and topmost branches in the foreground; at the end of the trunk (again the horizon is high up towards the top of the drawing) are the form of roots of the tree wrenched out of the ground pathetically dangling under a pallid sun. The branches of the tree in the foreground, by a strange metamorphosis, resemble a naked torso and limbs, the stripped branches seem as much human as arboreal. It is a curiously potent drawing charged with feeling so that it has an almost symbolic intensity. The sharp clarity of the pen drawn lines give it the vividness of a thing seen in a dream: yet it is utterly real, – the thing itself – invested with a poignancy that makes it an unforgettable image. Is it an oblique comment about the war in France and the deaths of many men? Or a configuring to himself of what his own fate might all too likely be? One can but speculate on its suggestiveness. He prized it, would not sell it, but gave it as a keepsake to his fiancée, Christine Kulenthal, when he went to the war. She kept it all her life.

The image of the fallen tree forms a recurrent image not only in John's work but also in that of Paul. John made a fine wood-engraving of a fallen tree seen from the same point of view as the pre-war drawing – from the branches, down the trunk to the root – as an illustration to *When thou wast naked* by T.F. Powys (Golden Cockerel Press 1931). For Paul, too, the fallen tree was the subject of photographs (in *Fertile Image*) a notable essay 'The Monster Field' published in *Outline* and in drawings and paintings. In the 1930s and 1940s the fallen tree is taken up by others influenced by the Nash brothers – most notably by Graham Sutherland in his etching entitled 'Pastoral' and in his 'Blasted Oak' drawing of 1941. John Craxton, too, following in the wake of the Nashes and of his mentor, Sutherland, made a whole series of drawings of tree roots in the estuary near Picton Castle in Pembrokeshire in 1943. As his drawings developed, the roots became less like roots and more like monsters, primeval beasts that had crawled from the water. But by 1943 Surrealism had made its impact: a tree was not a tree any longer.

In France (on the Belgian Front) John Nash was sent on a course at Oppy Wood – later to figure significantly as the subject for his largest war painting. In June 1917 he was made a Lance-Corporal, after which he was put through a number of tests to see if his courage and endurance were satisfactory and he was made a Corporal. He was ultimately made a Sergeant but he was unaware of his promotion till he returned to England in January 1918. Oppy Wood was supposed to be in a quiet sector of the Front, but this proved otherwise for it was constantly shelled. In June 1917 he was sent to the Front Line and went over the top on several occasions.

The fact that John Nash was at the Front for one year rather than for the duration of four years in no way diminishes the impact the horror and the carnage made on his sensitivity. It was bad enough to be surrounded by the death of countless nameless comrades whilst 'one was eating one's bully beef without bothering', but unbearable when a much beloved comrade was killed. Fortunately for John, already frustrated by his lack of promotion, Paul's influence and reputation as a war artist was exploited by him constantly on John's behalf. Paul appealed to Edward Marsh, Winston Churchill's Private Secretary and, through his good offices, John was withdrawn from the fighting. It is a mark of Paul's devotion not only to his brother, but to his sense of the intrinsic worth of his brother's art. John had to be removed from the Front: to be there meant that he could be maimed or killed. The loss to British Art would be irreparable. John was lucky. Late in January 1918 he came home on leave and was demobilised in February and commissioned as a Second Lieutenant in the Artists' Rifles in May so that he could wear officer's uniform, receive officer's pay and go back to the Western Front without let or hindrance if the need arose. There was no real need for him to do this, so he remained in Buckinghamshire, thereby missing the agonies of the final ghastly throes of the war.

The price of his withdrawal from the trenches was the painting of the War pictures. John had been able to make few sketches or drawings of the Western Front. Such practices would have been frowned upon by the authorities, so that much depended on the power and exactitude of his visual and emotional recall. The war experience had to be recreated imaginatively: but this, in some respects, was an advantage as the time-gap between the event and its recreation as a painting ensured that an objectivity and a directness were more readily achieved.

The work on the war pictures was carried out at Tubb's Farm in the village of Chalfont St. Peter near Gerrards Cross. The brothers had no studio as such and in any case wanted to be together in what was not unlike a joint enterprise in opening the eyes of the world to the reality of war, much as Siegfried Sassoon and Wilfred Owen had done in the unflinching realism of their poetry. Whatever else war might be, however necessary or unavoidable, it must be shown as it is, not obscured through a cloud of misplaced idealism. Of the two men, Paul's sense of moral indignation is the stronger. John's attitude is more objective. 'It was thus' his pictures seem to say, 'Make what you will of it'.

The sheer relief of not being in France is clearly shown in Paul's letter written 16 July 1918 to Gordon Bottomley:

> Jack and I are both temporarily seconded and employed by the Ministry of Information to paint pictures for records and propaganda, actually what we like, so long as it is interesting enough under these vague headings. To start off we have a large memorial painting to do and this is exercising our resources at the moment. My size is 10ft by something so I am going to be busy.... We have taken a large shed formerly used for drying herbs. It is roomy place with large windows down both sides, an ample studio – here we both work. Jack is lately married – a charming girl whom we all adore .... They live in rooms next to the shed and Bunty and I have a room in the old farm – a charming place with a wonderful cherry orchard and fine old barns & sheep & rabbits all that sort of thing. We all lunch together in the studio where there is a piano so our wives enchant us with music at times thro' the day. A phantastic existence as all lives seem these days but good while it lasts and should produce something worthwhile I suppose. France and the trenches would be a mere dream if our minds were not perpetually bent on those scenes. And yet how difficult it is, folded as we are in the luxuriant green country, to put it aside and brood on those wastes in Flanders, the torments, the cruelty and terror of this war. Well it is on *these* I brood for it seems the only justification of what I do now – if I can help to rob war of the last shred of glory, the last shine of glamour.

John's memorial picture 'Oppy Wood' was for him very large – six by seven feet – always a test of an artist's ability to control and articulate space. He faced the challenge by painting the evening light over a shattered wood – reduced now to a few shell-smashed trees standing over a trench from which two soldiers look out towards two shell bursts in the distance. Rothenstein calls it 'a peace rather than a war picture' and one can see why. The blueness of the sky, the peach-coloured clouds are in sharp contrast with the grassless earth below, and the leafless, fractured trees. There are no hurrying soldiers, no corpses nor mess. Despite the devastation, a kind of calm has descended on the scene pointing to the greater calm when the war will end. The ambiguity of effect that this picture creates is part of its meaning: on the ravaged fields and what were once woods, the waning day throws its last radiance. Where there was once the clamour of battle there is a stillness and calm. One day the grass will return, the trenches will be filled in, the trees throw out fresh branches and leaves and the barbed wire and corrugated iron will be carried away. For a moment, the evening light comes down like a benediction.

In contrast with this is the wartime masterpiece 'Over the Top' which is one of the very few pictures in the Ministry of Information's collection to depict a specific action – in this the last John had seen on active service. The event depicted took place early in the morning of 30 December 1917 at Welsh Ridge, Marcoing, south-west of Cambrai. The action undertaken was disastrous with 68 of the 80 officers and men killed. Fifty years on John wrote a letter to Joseph Darracott describing the action. 'It was in fact pure murder and I was lucky to escape untouched ... It was bitterly cold and we were easy targets against the snow and in day light ... I think the vivid memory of the occasion helped me when I painted the picture and provoked what intensity of feeling may be found in it.'

No picture could be more authentic. Its directness and its clarity of design immediately communicate its emotional power. Every component of the scene plays a dramatic part: the steeliness of the winter sky seems only to intensify the coldness of the snow; air and earth, so to speak, hostile to the men upon it. The trench that cuts along the base of the picture and up to the top left hand corner looks less like a trench and more like a great gash with jagged edges, a wound in the earth, its declivity offering not so much a shelter as a grave. From this the soldiers clamber, stumbling forward. The cumbersomeness of the postures of the figures communicates perfectly an action being carried out against well-nigh impossible odds – the painful slowness of advance for those still alive and the tragedy of the dead men prostrate in the snow at their feet. This is the more remarkable in so far as John Nash very rarely introduced figures into his pictures; the figures here are totally convincing.

In all, John Nash's output as an official war artist was six oil paintings and six finished drawings in pencil, pen, chalk and watercolours and a number of studies. 'Oppy Wood' and especially 'Over the Top' held pride of place. It would have been beyond his powers to maintain this high level of achievement in everything he produced. As it was, the 'bending of the mind on these scenes' took its own toll which had to find some sort of relief. Both brothers worked on their 'bloody war pictures' until six o'clock each evening. They were then free to turn to whatever they wanted to do – chiefly to paint a landscape which had been untouched by the horrible war. Fortunately for them, these landscapes lay at the backdoor of Tubb's Farm – or just beyond it.

It would be almost impossible to exaggerate the sense of relief experienced by returned soldiers at the end of the war. Siegfried Sassoon's poem 'Everyone sang' was essentially an expression of relief and a thankfulness for liberation from the war years.

> Everyone suddenly burst out singing:
> And I was filled with such delight
> As prisoned birds do find in freedom
> Winging over the white orchards and dark green fields
> On, on and out of sight....
> Oh and my heart was suddenly lifted...

The lifting of the heart finds memorable celebration in what was to prove John Nash's most famous picture, now in the Tate, 'The Cornfield'. The landscape depicted is near Chalfont St. Peter, the local Buckinghamshire countryside instinctively chosen to provide him with a scene that bespeaks calm plenitude: a hillside thick with corn, crowned with dark woods and suffused with the mellow light of a late afternoon at the end of summer. It is Keatsian in its intensity and suggestiveness. The masterly simplicity of the design, the formality and the boldness of the structure, the generous rhythms of the sweep of the land's contours and the sheaves of stooked corn – all the constituents working together compel one's admiration and wonder each time one sees it. It belongs with Traherne's

> The corn was orient and immortal wheat, which never should be reaped, nor was ever sown. I thought it stood from everlasting to everlasting.

Affirming life and growth after four years of death and disintegration, it testifies to a new found joy in living and the fulfilment promised in the forthcoming harvest. There can be little doubt that the painting of it afforded John Nash the necessary therapy of the spirit after the harrowing experiences of Flanders.

The mood of 'The Cornfield' also dominates the watercolour, 'French Landscape' painted about the same time and, as like as not, based on a landscape sketch made by John when he was off-duty behind the lines. (He told Rothenstein that 'behind the lines I did some pure landscape. *It was a means of saving my life*'.) Again the glow of the evening sun spreads across the landscape, 'plotted and pieced', which unfolds towards the base of the picture.

What is impressive is the way the design and colour in all their intimacy and warmth work together to communicate the harmonious spirit of the place. Like 'The Cornfield' it is a deeply felt painting. Again, it shares with 'The Cornfield' a visionary quality. Only an imaginative intensity of a high order and an emotional and spiritual pressure working under strict control could have produced works like these – and for all John Nash's later achievement, he never surpassed them.

John had married Christine Kulenthal in 1918 and after the first months spent in the room at the end of the former herb-drying shed, he and his wife moved in the autumn of 1919 to a flat above a chemist's shop in Gerrards Cross. Here they stayed for nearly two years, spending their first summer in Whiteleaf, Princes Risborough, the second in Sapperton in Gloucestershire. They knew that the flat was but a temporary expedient and so were relieved to move into Lane End House – a large cottage – at Meadle, a hamlet in the vale of Aylesbury. This was to be their home for the next twenty-two years, the base from which John would explore and paint the woods and hills of what was virtually his native county. In the expeditions to find suitable landscapes his wife played an important part. She had been trained at the Slade herself and was a painter of no small ability. With great unselfishness she gave up her own painting, working on the principle that one painter in the house was enough. Instead she walked and cycled hundreds of miles on 'reconnaissances' – 'reccys' as she called them. 'It was part of my job', she said, and added 'I do not want to boast but it was only the places I did not go to look at first that weren't successful'.

There now began what might rightly be termed the great Buckinghamshire series of John's paintings. It might be appropriate at this point to indicate that John Nash's paintings fall into two large groups regionally: the first the paintings of Buckinghamshire; the second of East Anglia. These two regions of Great Britain afforded him the landscapes that stimulated and engaged his creative powers. In his first period i.e. before he went to France as a soldier, his first landscapes were of the North Norfolk coast and hinterland followed by landscapes around his home at Iver Heath, the Misbourne Valley and Burnham Beeches near Slough. After the war his attention was largely focused on the hills of the Chilterns running down from

Wendover to the Thames Valley. Roughly speaking the area which most strikingly attracted him is the line of the ancient track of the Icknield Way which enters the county near Bledlow and, following the curve of the hills, moves north-eastwards leaving the country near the village of Edlesborough with its beautiful but now unused church. Churches never really interested or attracted John: roads, flowers, grass, woods did. Hence his response to the Traveller's Joy and the Wayfaring Tree to be found – in his day, at any rate – along the route taken by the Icknield Way above what were once the swamps of the plain and below the woods that clothed the chalk hills of the Chilterns.

East Anglia afforded a great contrast with the Buckinghamshire scenery. It lacked hills but made up for those by the quality of its light and space. Furthermore, there was the attraction of the coast and if, like the interior of East Anglia, the coast had little drama with its crumbling sandy cliffs, eaten into by the grey North Sea, the shingle beaches and their vegetation of sea-holly and wild pea, marram grass and sea lavender held attractions for him that were not to be lightly dismissed. And the one lesson that Claughton Pellew had impressed upon him was that there was no need to travel far for subject matter provided that the right sort of attention was brought to bear on, say, 'half a haystack'. That being said, throughout his life he always made painting trips to other parts of Great Britain to find fresh subjects so that he could avoid becoming sated and thus stale in both his response and his treatment. John and his wife travelled extensively out from their two centres of Meadle and Wormingford to Cornwall and Gloucestershire and to Skye; to Dorset and to the Gower Coast near Swansea; to Pembrokeshire and to the hills of Derbyshire; and to the docks of Bristol and Ipswich. The necessity for a fresh stimulus, a new challenge, quickened his spirit and it shows in his work. It is interesting to note here that he was always fascinated by ships and docks; he made drawings of these and paintings from these. Successful as these paintings are, they somehow seem extraneous to his committed theme: the lie of the land at all times and seasons.

Further variety of subject matter was provided by his botanical interests. His knowledge of plants (after all, trees were but 'the larger plants') and flowers went back further than the Botany Prize at Wellington and lasted the whole of his lifetime. There must be hundreds of drawings of flowers, made in all the stages of the plant's life from bud to seedhead. He seemed to grasp instinctively what Gwen John called the 'strange pose' of a plant or flower – the way a stem stands, a flower hangs or a leaf or frond curls. Usually he made drawings; but there are also oil paintings of flowers in a landscape, a particularly fine one being of Hellebores – 'that noble plant' – in a winter landscape as well as a number of flower pieces. Botanical drawing began in earnest after the move to Meadle. It is not without significance that it was at Lane End Cottage he first had a garden that he could call his own and which was to be of his own making.

It would be going too far to call Buckinghamshire John Nash's Promised Land, though his coming to live in it after the devastation of the war in France must have felt like a deliverance from a great peril. He was also newly-wed and had the satisfaction of being a married man in a house of his own. And, within little more than a stone's throw, a landscape on both sides of him – the Chiltern Hills and Aylesbury Plain – that was waiting, so it seemed, for an artist to interpret them.

There must be many watercolours and drawings that John made at this time, particularly of the beechwoods that grew on the tops of the Chilterns. Within walking or cycling distance, they offered such a varied range of views to the young artist that he was spoilt for choice. It was in Buckinghamshire that he started to paint the landscape in winter – unless one takes 'Over the Top' to be a significant precursor of the winter landscapes painted in the Chilterns and in Suffolk. He loved the season's capacity to transform totally the lines and textures of the land. He loved its whiteness and the way the whiteness threw into sharp relief the leafless boughs, the blackness of twigs and branches, the lines of the furrow, the darkness of a ditch of water overhung by dry bents of grass and rush. Similarly, in the Chilterns, he responded at once to the chalk outcrops and the chalk pits in the woods – the whiteness of the chalk with its blue-grey shadowings, and the limited specific plants that grew on it in the crevices and clefts enhanced the dramatic contrast with the overshadowing foliage and the smooth soaring trunks of the beech trees.

And he loved a good tree, too. Like his brother Paul, he too in his early days had made a drawing of the Wittenham Clumps seen from Sinodun House where his uncle lived. The Clumps had their own uniqueness and mystery which exerted a power over the boys, stimulating their imaginative response. Paul was to draw the Clumps time and again. They recur throughout his pictures, both oil paintings and water colours, like a significant recurring phrase of music. It is not therefore surprising to see John time and again returning to the image of the wood on the hilltop. But John's hilltop woods are themselves alone. They carry no symbolic overtones: their shapes, their branch and leaf movements inspiring the lines and patterning and shapes – all the elements of design coming together in the unity of his art. Nor only the wood on the hill's crest either. In 1913 he painted his first 'Path Through a Wood' and his fascination with the interiors of woods had begun. He is intrigued by the path that leads into the inner mysteries of the wood and as an image it recurs time and again in his paintings (and also in his wood-engravings). The assembly of trees creates for him a sort of structure of mystery, solitude and beauty: and though the odd minatory feeling is somehow there, it is never obtrusively there. For the wood's interior is a natural place for the spirit and as such is ingeniously explored and in that exploration there is a depth of cherishing. Not for nothing did he call one of his finest watercolours painted in the mid-1930s 'The Grove' with its pale grey central tree in a pose like a ritualist, a dancer participating in the mysteries of the grove. If one thinks of his paintings and drawings of wood interiors, one is reminded how much he shares in, say, a poet like Kipling's intense and indelible awareness of the significance of the woods in the English landscape – the last remaining (though threatened) centres of calm, oases of the spirit. The mood the pictures evoke is akin to:

> They shut the road to the woods
> Seventy years ago.
> Weather and rain have undone it again,
> And now you would never know
>
> There once was a road through the woods
> Before they planted the trees
> It is underneath the coppice and heath
> And the thin anemones....

Such haunted moments do not come often, credibly, in either poems or paintings.

It is interesting to note how he modifies his drawings of the Buckinghamshire trees in the years between 1919 and 1936. The element of patterning is stressed in the early watercolours. The arrangements of shapes made by branch and leaf frond is simplified into a design: a bough of leaves becomes a banner-shaped form – and the whole is emphasised by much fine and detailed pen work which gives a sharpness of emphasis linking the early work of the late 'teens and early 'twenties with the pre-war work (1912 to 1915/16). This is considerably modified during the late 1920s and the early 1930s. The pen is replaced by the pencil, cross-hatching is eschewed, and the forms are simply painted in tones of great subtlety. One has only to compare 'The Grove' which was painted in the Chiltern Woods in the mid-1930s with the earlier 'Whiteleaf Woods' or the 'Interior of a Wood' to see the advance in delicacy and subtlety his art has made. The rhythms are less assertive; but nonetheless movingly felt.

His reputation in the 1920s and 1930s rested largely on his Chiltern paintings. As a consequence, he was invited by Jack Beddington, Publicity Manager of Shell-Mex and BP, to write and illustrate the Shell Guide for Buckinghamshire. (Paul had written and illustrated the Shell Guide to Dorset.) The Buckinghamshire Shell Guide came out in 1937 with John's engaging text, his exquisite end-papers with a design of falling beech leaves, his notes on the buildings of interest and distinction, and a chapter on the flora of the county illustrated with appropriate botanical drawings. Apart from the fact that the book was a means of earning money (for the Nashes were poor in the 1930s) it gave John the opportunity to write and have his writing published. Though he never became 'a man of letters', one glimpses in this book the kind of writer he might well have become had impulses and circumstances been different. If more was needed than his paintings and drawings to confirm how fascinated he was by trees it can be found in this passage about Burnham Beeches:

> Burnham Beeches are unlike any other beech woods in the country, for the trees have been pollarded and have grown to the most fantastic shapes and sizes with immense trunks, gnarled and decaying. They cover undulating ground which is crossed by several wellkept gravel drives, which contrast strangely with the terrifying aspect of the trees.

And even livelier and more lyrical:

> But it is to the beech woods in mid-Bucks that the county owes its reputation. Winter is by no means the least beautiful of the seasons in the woods. The sun turns the carpet of dead leaves to pale red and orange, over which the intricate shadows of the tree trunks and branches curve and dip with every rise and fall of the ground. Or on a dull day, after rain a blue mist hangs in the woods, changing the leaves to a dark red through which the red soil shows in black rifts. The smooth green pillars of the beech trees streaked in black stand in endless quiet arcades. In Spring there is more movement, the trees wear sweeping dresses, trail flounces, carry parasols of shrill acid green. The play of light on these complicated lacy masses of foliage is bewildering. Full summer seems heavy and quiet between the brilliance of Spring and Autumn: then the range of colours becomes extravagant, the woods are a conflagration of reds, browns and burning orange till the fire dies out and the skeletons of winter trees emerge again.

The richness and authenticity of the response to the woods throughout the year is marvellous, arising as it does from the precision of description, the accumulation of sensuous detail controlled into a rhythmic and changing design. 'The greatest mystery comes from the greatest definition' wrote Gordon Bottomley to John's brother, Paul. As in painting and drawing, so in writing the very spirit of the beech woods is perfectly established in the reader's mind. The writing is of a piece with the painting and is one more instance of the feeling that John Nash (like his brother) had for the spirit of the place, the genuine love. When his feeling for the spirit of the place was right, the paintings were a success. But then, he rarely embarked on a drawing or painting of a place unless it moved him.

One might think that during the Meadle period his preoccupation with the hills and trees precluded other aspects of Buckinghamshire. Not so. Looking down from the Ridge, his eye travelled over the Aylesbury Plain consisting of rich, undulating pasture and lands broken by ranges of low hills and watered by innumerable streams. There exist several paintings of the Plain: and as in any paintings of flat country the sky plays a more significant role than the land. In 'The Edge of the Plain' and in the painting entitled, 'Meadle, The Vale of Aylesbury' the artist's preoccupation with cloud formation is what impresses the onlooker. For John Nash this is unusual: he is happier with the earth and water, which is perhaps why he usually places his horizon high in the picture. It is not simply a technical device. He can get better spatial effects with the land in all its variety. The light and air are, 'skied' in most of his work. Ultimately, it is the hills and woods that remain memorable: the great vault of the sky is something beyond his creative powers. Its vast airy limitlessness which makes itself felt in flat areas both challenges and defeats him: better the near, the intimate, the 'firm-set' earth and the ripple of water in the reeds, the here and now of the pheasants in the snow.

During the years he lived at Meadle, John Nash accomplished a great deal of work besides his painting. Sometime in late 1918 or early 1919 he taught himself to become a wood-engraver for at Christmas 1919 he sent to Paul and his sister-in-law, Bunty, (Margaret Nash) a Christmas present, a small folio of twelve engravings he had made earlier in the year, the first fruits of a craft in which he was to prove a distinguished practitioner. Little is known who taught him even the rudiments of this craft. It is possible that Paul and his friend, Rupert Lee, may have given him the original inspiration to engage in what is a very skilled undertaking. It could not have been Claughton Pellew for he did not start wood-engraving until about 1923. The practice of the craft was 'in the air' by the 1920s and was to flourish, thanks to its use by the private presses, until the Second World War which put an end to such undertakings. In 1921 he became a member of the Society of Wood-Engravers. It was at Meadle where he made his outstanding series of wood-engravings for 'Poisonous Plants', one of the most important of the Haslewood Books published by Etchells and MacDonald. He continued to make wood engravings throughout the 1920s until the early 1930s when in 1934 he ended his 'wood-chopping' career by making what were to be his last and, it has been claimed, his finest wood engravings to illustrate 'Flowers and Faces' published in 1935 by the Golden Cockerel Press. The ungrateful author, H.E. Bates, told him, astonishingly, at a publisher's party, that he had ruined the book. Whether this unsettled John or not, or whether he felt he had done enough 'wood-chopping' (he had, after all, made over 140 engravings!) he made no more wood-engravings, choosing to work in line drawing or lithography.

Between 1919 and 1939 he illustrated about thirty books, ranging from the comic illustrations for Lance Sieveking's books in 1919 to the lithographs and drawings in 1939 that so sympathetically accompany Adrian Bell's 'Men and the Fields' ('It is one of those 9/6d bargains that still make one gasp' wrote Pat Gilmour. 'Nash's patient stippling and subtle adjustment of the transparent colours of yellow and cyan with rose pink and grey erring towards warmth, achieve the suggestion of infinitely more colour, particularly lovely in the lilac-russet of some trees ... or where a pot-bellied bee hangs by a brilliant orange snapdragon'.) He also illustrated the catalogue of Alpine and Herbaceous Plants for his friend and fellow plantsman, Clarence Elliott (a hundred of which he and Christine coloured by hand) and made many line drawings of flowers. He also made coloured lithographs of flowers for his friend Robert Gathorne-Hardy's *Wild Flowers of Britain*. His achievement as a book-illustrator has been splendidly dealt with by his friend John Lewis in *John Nash: the painter as illustrator* and by Clare Colvin in her detailed study *John Nash: Book Designs*, the catalogue of the exhibition held at the Minories, Colchester, in 1986. After the war, John Nash was to continue making book illustrations more or less until just before his death in 1977.

From 1924 to 1929 John also taught at the Ruskin School of Art in Oxford under Sidney Carline, an artist who trained at the Slade and showed with the London Group and was eager to share his ideas with his colleague. It is difficult to know just how much Carline's ideas and practices affected John Nash's own work. John, who had received no formal art school training and who worked largely by intuition guided by the sincerity and innocence of his instinctive response, made what he could of his preceptor's theory and practice. But it is likely that the changes that one notices in his painting during the two interwar decades may well have had their first promptings from Carline. After Sidney Carline's death in 1929, John did not teach again until 1934 when he was appointed by William Rothenstein, Principal of the Royal College of Art, to be Assistant Teacher of Design at the College, a post he held until 1957 – apart from the war years when he was on active service.

The last five years of the 1930s were, however, profoundly saddened by the death of his son, William, in a car accident. The little boy was seated beside his mother who was driving, when the door on the passenger side flew open. Christine held on to the boy as long as she could, but needed both hands to control the car. The child slipped from her hands and hit his head on the kerbstone. He was killed by the blow. John blamed his wife for the tragedy and loss and was slow to forgive her, for he was deeply devoted to his son. He always kept William's books which he had delightfully illustrated.

If he was slow to forgive, his recovery was slow too. How much his work was affected by William's death can only be conjectured. At the end of the 1930s he experienced what many artists feel after a sustained creative effort over twenty years. He began to feel 'played out' and that he could no longer undertake with his former relish the fresh challenge offered to him by new landscapes. His son's death only aggravated the problem which is a common enough one in all creative people. In his inmost being he knew that if there was to be any continuity, not to speak of development, he needed a fallow period. Events in Europe were now moving to their ominously tragic conclusion with the declaration of war in September 1939 and this gave him, ironically enough, the respite from painting and illustration his spirit needed.

In view of his outstanding contribution to the war paintings of the 1914–18 war, he was made an 'Official War Artist, this time attached to the Navy'. The assignment was not a success. In 1940 and 1941 he served as a War Artist in Plymouth, Bristol and Swansea, making drawings of docks, ships and submarines. But his heart was not in it and he knew it. His integrity was such that he knew that he did not want to live with this false position. He had had his say about war with painful immediacy in 'Over the Top' and 'Oppy Wood'. Though he produced a number of paintings and drawings from his service as an Official War Artist, they do not rank amongst his memorable works: they have, at best, a marginal importance. It was to his relief that he could turn his back on drawing and painting when he was commissioned in the Royal Marines and went on active service serving in Rosyth, Dover and Portsmouth. In November 1944 he was discharged with the rank of Temporary Captain. The three year break from being an artist could not have proved more beneficial. Probably more than anything else, the lucky accident of the war enabled him to resume painting with fresh enthusiasm. After all, his life as painter was but half over. The 'fresh woods and pastures new' of Suffolk and north Essex had beckoned him since 1929 when he first stayed at Wormingford. With the chance to buy a house in the Stour Valley he was able to bid farewell to Buckinghamshire. 'Tomorrow' had arrived.

It is misleading to suggest that the 1929 visit to Suffolk was John Nash's first acquaintance with East Anglia. There had been walking holidays in Norfolk with Claughton Pellew before the First World War and in 1919 the charming watercolour of Dunwich with its naked male bathers eyed apprehensively by the ladies on a slightly removed shoal of shingle bears witness to his acquaintance with the area. But it was a patron of John's, Sir Montague Pollock, living at Beaconsfield who told John that Suffolk might well provide him with a variety of landscapes that he would find to stimulate his interest. So, from 1929 and through the 1930s the Nashes visited Suffolk, renting bungalows and cottages in the summer. Thus the East Anglia experience overlaps increasingly with the Buckingham years although what was to prove a forty-year-old love affair with East Anglia was not ratified and consummated until the Nashes moved into Bottemgoms in 1945.

Lane End House was sold. The Nashes had not lived there since the outbreak of the war and it had been let to five different sets of tenants. It was a relief to sell the house: but what they were to undertake appeared to be daunting. Christine Nash's account of the first encounter with Bottemgoms is too good to miss:

> I knew it for years before we lived here. I used to see it from the track down below when we rented a cottage by the river. But I'd never approached it by the road until 1943 when a friend told us it might be possible to buy it. The farmer who owned it had had it standing empty for eight years, and he had come to the conclusion that a few hundred pounds was really more valuable to him than just to see it falling into decay. So I came by Chambers' bus from Colchester and walked down the track, which in those days was a leafy bower, with the hedges meeting overhead, so one walked through a tunnel of greenery. As I walked, I saw an old man coming up the track with a bag over his shoulder, and a stick. We stopped and said Goodmorning, and he said, 'I'm the postman. My name is Death'. That was a very good opening. I went on down past the house, which was actually impossible to get near to. The nettles and elders were right up to the top of the ground floor windows. There was no trace of a garden, no sign of a path. So I continued down the track and sat for a long time under a willow tree by a barn and I thought it was the most beautiful place I'd ever seen, but absolutely impossible to contemplate as a house to live in. The idea of reclaiming it, and maintaining it even if we could reclaim it, seemed even more formidable. I must have stayed there under the willow tree at least an hour before, very regretfully, I walked back up the leafy track.

The acquisition of the house and the land surrounding it was, as near as makes no difference, a fresh beginning. The restoring of the house just sufficiently to make it habitable and no more fell largely on Christine's shoulders while John and friends and helpers from Wormingford cut down and tamed the jungle of nettles and elders and set about creating the garden of his dreams in the rich and fertile soil. So the old neglected place became new again, brought back to life from the edge of dereliction. More than that, it became a home, a centre. John used to refer to Bottemgoms as 'the old homestead' for that is what it became: the centre he always started from and to which he always returned.

Nor did he need to go far from it in search of subjects, for he recorded it time and again at all times and in all seasons: the track coming down to the end of the domain in summer, and again in the snow: the ponds lost behind the bamboos and gunneras in July and then stripped naked in the January frost. The black barn, the Blenheim weighed down with apples in September. The landscape at his doorstep or from his L-shaped studio window upstairs afforded him an endless variety of motifs – it was inexhaustible, and there must be hundreds of paintings in oil, watercolour and monochrome which do nothing less than celebrate the sheer wonder of his being alive in such a place. In that moving essay that DH Lawrence wrote towards the end of his life, 'Hymns in a man's life', he says that what ails twentieth-century man is his boredom, the world for modern man isn't wonderful any more. 'We have lost our sense of wonder'. But John Nash never lost his sense of wonder at the natural world and his wonder is registered in his drawings and paintings. Furthermore, he knew that if ever the wonder of life eluded him in his work then his work was dead at once, lacking animation and necessary vitality and so worthless.

The habits of a lifetime stood him in good stead. He had trained himself from boyhood to be a good observer. His friend, Natalie Barclay, recounts that a walk in the country with him was a revelation: things that had been seen a hundred times and never properly noticed were seen afresh – he simply opened your eyes to the wonder of the commonplace in landscape and flowers. Related to this sharpness and sensitivity of observation is the quality of concentration he manages to get into his finest landscapes. He immediately seizes on the pattern that will bring the various elements of a landscape into a coherent whole – he would, if pressed, refer to these as the abstract qualities of a landscape – by which he meant the vital relationship of specific natural forms. It did not do to pursue this line of thought too remorselessly with him. It was an intuitive gift he knew he had and one which he knew would not be helped by art-theoretical probing. But it was unmistakably there in his best pictures and it is what gives them their especial qualities of freshness, unity and unequivocal directness.

It is this reluctance to 'talk about art' that makes it hard to come to grips with the work of others that had an influence on him. No artist can work in total isolation and what we know of John Nash is that his admiration for the work of Edward Lear never really left him. The clarity and harmony of Lear's landscapes make themselves felt particularly in the watercolours of the late 1930s and 1950s and 1960s. And it has to be remembered that as a young man in his late 'teens and early 'twenties he was much moved and influenced by the watercolours of Girtin, Cotman, Cozens and De Wint which he saw at the Victoria and Albert Museum. How much he *studied* them we shall never know: but it must always be remembered that he was well aware that to a degree they shaped and moulded his work. Certainly the magic of watercolours fascinated him, its transparency and unlaboured immediacy held a charm that oil painting rarely achieved.

'Nevertheless', wrote DH Lawrence, 'landscapes can be very lovely, especially in watercolour which is a more bodiless medium and does not aspire to any substantial existence, and is so small it does not try to make a deep seizure on the consciousness. Watercolour will always be more of a statement than an experience. Hence the English have delighted in landscape and have succeeded in it well .... For more than a century we have produced delicious watercolours....'. Lawrence's recognition that the English genius accommodated itself through the medium of watercolours is particularly true of John Nash. He was instinctively drawn to use it from the first and whatever he absorbed from seeing the work of the masters of English watercolour both in the museums and in reproduction in magazines and books at home is to be found in the work produced throughout his life. How systematic his study was we can but conjecture.

What we do know is that he submitted himself to the paintings and allowed them to work their own way on him. It was not a very conscious process; much more was it akin to being 'felt in the blood and felt along the heart'.

As he received no formal art instruction, he learned from others: there was no other way. In addition to the work of the great watercolourists of the past he observed what his brother painted and what his brother's artist friends produced. From an amalgam of influences like these his own especial gift was conditioned, modified and shaped. Conscious of his lack of training throughout his life, he was always ready ot listen and to learn. But the process must not go too far. His unswerving fidelity was to his own daemon.

As a painter in oils he was particularly grateful for the help he received from Harold Gilman and Charles Ginner. They did all within their power to remedy his lack of technical knowledge in oil paintings and he proved a ready and apt pupil. It is remarkable that 'Over the Top' and 'The Cornfield' were painted by a young man of twenty-five who had started using oils only six years before. Later, in the 1920s, when he taught at the Ruskin School in Oxford with Sidney Carline, he listened to and, to some degree, absorbed Carline's elaborate theories of tone and technique. But no really radical change took place in his manner or approach as a consequence. Later still, after 1944 he would go on painting holidays with Edward Bawden and Carel Weight and, although he worked side by side with these artists, his techniques had by then settled down to being unchangeably and inalienably his own.

Mention must be made too of his acquaintance with the French School. Oddly enough, he saw neither of the Post-Impressionist exhibitions – presumably he was at school at the time of the first; but it is amazing that when he was beginning to consider being an artist, he did not visit the second, especially as the circle of friends he shared with Paul must have seen it and talked much about it. But no, he missed it and his chance to see much French art in English collections was very limited. It was not until he encountered the work of Lhote, Vlaminck and particularly

Jean Marchand in the collection of Percy Moore-Turner that he saw continental work that related to his own. What attracted him was the simplification of forms in a landscape which enhanced their significance. It was this quality that he subsequently endeavoured to achieve in his own painting so that the rhythms of the land's contours could be meaningfully realised. But it would be difficult to sustain the claim that even this first-hand acquaintance with French painting profoundly altered John Nash's innate vision and design.

Nor did it much affect his use of colour. After Paul's death, when he was clearing up his brother's studio, he noticed how limited was Paul's range of colours and he confessed that neither he nor his brother had been great colourists. They had both been from the first scrupulous about using the best quality paints in both oil and watercolour. But a vivid and dramatic sense of colour was not to be found in their pictures. John always said that he wished he had the eye and the daring for bolder and more brilliant, living colour. Yet, if he had risked all on a brighter, more superficially arresting palette, it would somehow be totally out of character. His natural reticence, his gift for understatement and his fidelity to his subject, all these would have precluded it in art as well as in life. It simply was not his style.

In any case, he made his mark; for honours came upon him in mid- and later life. In 1940 he was made an Associate of the Royal Academy (despite Paul's disapproval of that Institution) and in 1957 he was elected as a Royal Academician. In 1964 he was awarded the CBE. But what gave him especial pleasure was the fact that he was the first Academician to be given a large retrospective exhibition in five of its galleries at Burlington House in 1967. He was then in his mid-seventies and the pictures were at odds with the preoccupations of the moment – Pop Art, Abstraction, the impact of American painting. Unsurprisingly, the critical assessment was mixed: but the effect on his subsequent sales was tonic (though he never pushed up his prices) and dealers like Stanley Hardy, David Wolfers and Anthony d'Offay knew that the time had come to re-introduce John Nash's work to a younger generation of collectors, especially those committed to the English achievement in painting between the two World Wars. With this Indian summer of success, his work at the Royal Academy's Summer Show was always sought after. Though his early paintings commanded quite high prices in the London galleries, his current work was sold at the most modest of prices, thus encouraging younger collectors whose means were more limited. He was urged and encouraged by his friend, RA Bevan, to put up his prices for his Academy paintings, but he never would. A collector once visiting the Nashes at Bottemgoms to buy a painting from John, told him how much he had delighted in his work since first seeing it as a schoolboy in *Picture Post* with John Rothenstein's accompanying essay. After reading the essay, he resolved that if ever he had the money he would buy a painting. Forty years on, this he had done from a London gallery. 'I do not want to be unduly inquisitive' said Christine, hesitant but quite determined, 'but may I ask how much you paid for it?' The collector apparently moved from foot to foot uneasily and then disclosed the sum. 'I think, dear,' she said, 'You'd better come to see *us* in the future. I am sure it would be to your advantage'. 'And', the collector said, 'It was.' At the most modest of prices young collectors were able to buy enchanting work – leaves from the sketchbooks when the landscape depicted had been used for larger works or oils, squared-up drawings and drawings for book illustrations were all grist to the collector's mill. Though not 'finished' in the technical sense, these sheets from the sketchbooks have an unlaboured freshness and clarity. The watercolour sketch 'catches the joy as it flies' and for that reason alone is specially treasured. There were, however, exceptions. What remained of his early work was either put well away from the sight of collectors and dealers as he had so little of it, or it was, by comparison with his other work, more expensive though not devastatingly so. It would also be a fortunate collector who managed to get him to part with his precious botanical drawings. Only the 'dear ones' (his local, immediate circle of close friends) ever had the right credentials to obtain a drawing or painting of flowers. Not until he felt he could hold on to them no longer – two years before he died – was he persuaded by Anthony d'Offay to part with a sufficiency of them to make up an exhibition at d'Offay's gallery. This was most aptly commemorated by the publication of John's only published autobiographical statement *The Artist Plantsman* where, as one reads, one hears clearly the very cadences of his voice in the formal, rather studied style.

Being an academician also shaped his year in that much time and thought was given to what were to be his Academy pictures. Here his sketch book proved invaluable and he was enabled to choose and concentrate from a range of landscape studies. It was this work that formed the basis of his income. In addition, there were books to be illustrated, teaching to be done at Bigwood and finally at Flatford, Chelsea to visit, the garden to be attended to and sketching expeditions from Cornwall to Skye to be embarked upon. There were certain regular patterns in the day or the month that never changed. He always worked systematically and would have no truck with those who 'wouldn't work'. His art and his garden shaped his day; what was left of it went on fishing – an early passion – and music, for both he and his wife were good musicians and, until arthritis wrecked his hands, John and Christine would play duets on their handsome Steinway grand. He played an important part in the Aldeburgh Festivals attending concerts, decorating programmes and enjoying exhibitions of his work and the work of fellow East Anglian and other artists. Among his many musician friends he was happy to number Benjamin Britten and Lennox Berkeley: in fact one can justifiably say that his friendship with gardeners, fishermen and musicians afforded him a respite and a pleasure. For though a solitary man, he loved company. He liked parties and his trips to Academy functions, just as during the war he had enjoyed the camaraderie of the Officers' Mess. It was a relief from painting and a relief from himself. Though he could be witty and humorous, it was a dry, rather understated wit that marked him out and in a way, though he was often alone in his studio for hours on end, he liked to seek out the company of 'dear ones'. Never very far away was 'The Black Dog', the constitutional periodic melancholy and depression which seized upon him from time to time, oppressing his spirits and unsettling his health. Could this strain of nerves and spirit have been inherited from his mother's depressive state? It seems likely. It humbugged him periodically throughout his life and he was often hard pressed to find an effective strategy to counteract it. His art threw him back on himself. Nearly all his landscapes are unpeopled while the comic drawings are crowded with them. Hence his need for others who would stay him with food, conversation and, in many instances, love. Solitude oppressed him as it never did Christine. So there had to be people for companionship. It did not much matter who it was or whether the companionship was of a moment or more enduring – the postman, one of the farm workers passing down the field track, the children from the farm at the top of the road, Marion Benham, the Berkeleys – the brief or longer talk was instrumental in keeping the insidious melancholy at bay.

Which is where it is best, perhaps, to leave him.

It is Winter. The afternoon light has drained out of the yellow-grey sky, harbinger of snow. He has been making drawings of seed heads propped up in a jamjar. But now the shadows are thickening in the L-shaped studio with its disappearing northern light and it is time to stop work. Downstairs the fire is lit in the sitting room and the prospect of Ronald Blythe coming to visit, to talk, to read ... to enjoy, in short, that communality without which art cannot easily flourish, nor the spirit, no matter how deeply touched, find a home.

Rosa Centifolia Moschata Crestata

'The Artist Plantsman'

John Nash (Anthony d'Offay, 1976)

When I was about eight years old my family left London for the country where my father had built a house at Iver Heath in Buckinghamshire. Although we found ourselves suddenly among the novel delights and excitements of the country, we were not strangers to rural pursuits, as for many years we had accompanied my father when he went partridge-shooting at my uncle's farm near Wallingford. These occasions were unique and remained long in my memory. Here were all the comforts of the Edwardian scene, soon to disappear in the 1914–1918 war. Servants in caps and aprons rustled into prayers before breakfast, and again at bedtime, for the uncle was a man of strict religious principles. Everything came from the farm, from the delicious bread and abundant fruit to the home-cured Berkshire ham. In a large yard behind the house a donkey, urged on by a small boy, worked a pump on an endless circular track to supply water for the house. Peaches blushed behind netting on the enclosing walls. The house itself raised its hideous Victorian proportions at the end of a long ascending drive, shut in by orchards, the trees laden with September riches. Horticulturally I can only connect the garden with the precise pegged-down Verbenas, Sweet Scabious and the striped and gilded trumpets of Salpiglossis. In the distance the Sinodun ridge, on which my uncle's home stood, rose to the Wittenham Clumps, a landmark of great significance to my brother and myself.

My knowledge and interest in plants was stimulated by an excellent governess, whose services we shared with a neighbour's children. Her predecessor had been dismissed by my father after being caught teaching me a false quantity in Latin. But the second one was strongly approved of by us, being nearer our age and keen and stimulating on country matters. Down the road there were five maiden ladies, whose garden was a delight and where again we came in for instruction of a gentle nature. Each old lady still preserved her own childhood plot apart from the main garden, and the somewhat unkempt box-edged borders were full of 'treasures'.

At home I thought to take our own garden in hand. It had never been planned and contained few plants except some rosebeds edged with Mrs Sinkins Pinks. Father's full-size croquet lawn dominated everything and money was not forthcoming for the purchase of new plants. A lasting memory was a colony of Campanula rapunculoides, wisely imprisoned between the morningroom wall and the path, while Eccremocarpus scaber ran into a Gloire de Dijon nearby. I still have this latter combination in my garden today. At about this time of disillusionment with home gardening I went in for the Botany Prize at Wellington, in order to avoid compulsory cricket. Some sport had to be played and I chose Fives. With freedom to ramble and collect specimens, I spent two agreeable Summer Terms. There were only three contestants for the Prize, which I carried off by a process of elimination!

After Wellington my gardening fervour seems to have waned until I married and became a garden owner on the edge of the Aylesbury Plain, below the Chiltern escarpment. By now I must have acquired quite a knowledge of plants through reading, visiting friends' gardens and drawing such plants as I attempted to cultivate. Catalogues, which were sent gratis in those days, were eagerly studied, and kept one in touch with gardening topics. I used to keep all mine in the earth-closet at the end of the garden where they came in for constant study. One catalogue particularly attracted my attention, for instead of the usual bald and arid description of plants, there were hints of romance and a sly humour. From this Six Hills Nursery I ordered an Alpine plant notoriously difficult to grow. The plant belied the name on the label and some miserable usurper appeared. I complained and received apologies with a replacement. Impressed by this courtesy, I sent the manager a small wood engraving of Bee Orchis. This was the beginning of a long friendship with the Nurseryman, Plant Collector or, as he preferred it, 'Gardener', Clarence Elliott, and was an introduction to a vastly extended world of horticulture, where Elliott knew everyone. I used to draw the plants he had collected on his expeditions to the Andes and the Falkland Islands and elsewhere, not excluding finds in English gardens, which he maintained were the best hunting-ground. I was always at the ready to visit Stevenage if something special happened, such as the first flowering after several years of Puya alpestris, and I remember the agony of helping to replant it in more commodious quarters, the leaves being furnished with thorns facing in two directions.

I wrote articles for *Gardening Illustrated* and attended the Chelsea Flower Shows, where I would be allotted the Alpine or Herbaceous Plants, or more often, the 'New and Rare'. This particular tent had an almost holy atmosphere about it. One tiptoed in with feelings of high expectancy. Very few other people were there, the big marquees flaunting their vast displays drew off all but the dedicated plantsmen. Here were plants straight from outlandish habitats, the fruits of the intrepid collector. Here also were the new 'cultivars', (a term then unused), painfully reared over long periods by single-minded horticulturists.

The first book I illustrated was the Six Hills Nursery catalogue, a hundred copies of which my wife and I coloured by hand. This was a whim of C.E.'s and, looking back, I feel must have severely strained the Nursery's finances. The following year, in 1927, *Poisonous Plants* was published, with twenty-two of my wood engravings.

The actual title of the book was *Poisonous Plants: Deadly, Dangerous and Suspect*. The publishers thought that someone 'with a name' should be asked to write an introduction but in the end Dr Hill, Director of Kew, merely lent his name and delegated the plant descriptions to a member of his staff. I was left to write the introduction myself which gave me the added pleasure of being both artist and author. *Plants with Personality* (1938) was one of the books I particularly enjoyed illustrating. The subjects were dictated and specimens mostly sent to me to draw – a very hazardous business – Tibouchina semi-decandra was sent three times in ladies' stays boxes before a reasonable specimen sustained the post. In *English Garden Flowers* (1948) the choice of subjects was my own, as well as the written parts. *The Tranquil Gardener* (1958) and *The Native Garden* (1961) by Robert Gathorne-Hardy benefitted from the close and understanding collaboration which long friendship and conformity of tastes produce. *The Curious Gardener*, *The Contemplative Gardener* and *The Tranquil Gardener*, their moods follow on very properly, and the artist should be content to accompany them. Further titles on these lines would be hard to invent – tranquillity has the last word.

For many years I conducted a course on Plant Illustration at the Flatford Mill Field Centre. This started chiefly with the ideal of drawing the British Flora, but a visit to a local garden full of rare bulbs and herbaceous 'exotica' led to defections from the original purpose. There was no wish to spurn the humbler forms of our native flora, but they stood a poor chance against the riches of colour and the wealth of form provided by the garden exotics. We wanted to draw our plants with some freedom, giving them air and light and even decorative values, but at the same time to conform to the title of our course. The distinction between a good and a bad plant drawing is hard to make. If you look at the plant draughtsman's Bible, Wilfred Blunt's *Botanical Illustration*, you will find some illustrations which conform to the need for accuracy combined with the spark of a live drawing, as well as much work which may serve its purpose but gives no feeling of the living subject.

For nearly seventy years I have drawn plants for love or necessity and have never destroyed even slight sketches or notes in case they should be needed for reference (publishers can have an awkward habit of asking for illustrations in the 'dead' season). In any case, I feel a slight pencil flourish even of part of a plant is more valuable than a photograph. The open innocent countenance of a Daisy or Anemone may seem easy to draw, but they too can prove to be a snare, and sometimes I prefer the hooded Labiates, helmeted Monkshood and Balsam, or the leering countenance of Foxglove and Pentstemon.

October 1976

Trees by the Sea, Norfolk. 11″ × 10¼″
Watercolour and ink. Signed, not dated, but c 1913; Anthony d'Offay Gallery

The Garden at Wood Lane House. 12¼" × 17½"
Ink. Not signed c 1912; Private Collection

Iver Heath. 10¼″ × 15″
Watercolour and ink. Signed c 1913; Spink and Son

Trees in a Flood. 16¼″ × 13¼″
Watercolour and ink. Signed c 1913; Leeds City Art Gallery

The Three Carts. 8″ × 6¾″
Ink. Not signed c 1914; Private Collection

Misbourne Valley. 7¼″ × 9¾″
Watercolour and pencil. Signed and inscribed c 1915; Private Collection

The Fallen Tree. 6¾″ × 5″
Watercolour and ink. Not signed, but dated 1915; Private Collection

A Bombing Post in the Snow. 10¼" × 18"
Watercolour and ink. c 1918; Trustees of the Imperial War Museum, London

Dunwich. 10″ × 15″
Watercolour and ink. Signed and dated 1919; Spink and Son

Sunlight and Shadow: Trees in the Chilterns. 8½″ × 9¾″
Ink. Signed and dated 1920; Buckinghamshire County Museum

Chalford, Gloucestershire. 13¾″ × 16½″
Pencil and wash. Signed and dated 1920; Private Collection

Wittenham Clumps, from Sinodun House
Watercolour and pencil. Signed, not dated, but c 1913

45

A Game of Croquet. 8¾″ × 11¼″
Watercolour and ink. Signed and dated 1913; Spink and Son

About a pig. 11″ × 15″
Watercolour and ink. Not signed, but dated 1913; Spink and Son

Gloucestershire Landscape. 19″ × 23½″
Oil. Signed and dated 1914; Ashmolean Museum, Oxford

Hillside at Night (Starry Night). 9⅜″ × 12⅝″
Watercolour. Not signed, but dated 1914; Spink and Son

Tuscan Landscape. 14″ × 15″
Watercolour and ink. Signed and dated 1914; Spink and Son

Slough Pools. 17″ × 14⅝″
Watercolour, chalk and ink. Signed and dated 1915; Private Collection

Meon Valley. 10″ × 10¾″
Watercolour and pencil and chalk. Signed and dated 1915; Private Collection

52

The Thunderstorm (The Monks' Field). 11½″ × 15″
Watercolour. Signed c 1915; Private Collection

Threshing. 30″ × 25″
Oil. Signed and dated 1915; Private Collection

54

The Threshing Machine. 15¾″ × 22½″
Watercolour and ink. Signed and dated 1914; Private Collection

The Viaduct. 35″ × 26″
Oil. Not signed. Dated 1915–16; Leeds City Art Gallery

Oppy Wood, 1917, Evening. 72″ × 84″
Oil. Signed and dated 1918; Trustees of the Imperial War Museum, London

57

Over the Top: 1ˢᵗ Artists' Rifles at Marcoing. 31¼″ × 42¼″
Oil. Signed and dated 1918; Trustees of the Imperial War Museum, London

The Cornfield. 27″ × 30″
Oil. Signed and dated 1918; Trustees of the Tate Gallery, London

French Landscape. 14″ × 15″
Watercolour and pencil. Signed and dated 1918; Spink and Son

The Edge of the Orchard. 10¾″ × 12¼″
Watercolour and ink. Signed and dated 1919; Private Collection

Interior of a Wood, Whiteleaf. 14½″ × 14¼″
Watercolour and ink. Signed and dated 1919; Spink and Son

Summer in Whiteleaf Woods. 10¾″ × 14¾″
Watercolour and ink. Signed and dated 1919; Buckinghamshire County Museum

The Timber Stack, Chiltern Woods. 10¾″ × 15¼″
Watercolour and ink. Signed and dated 1920; Leicestershire Museums and Art Galleries

The Cornfield, Wiston, Suffolk. 15½″ × 22″
Oil. Signed and dated 1920; Private Collection

Hillside, Whiteleaf. 20½″ × 14½″
Watercolour and ink. Signed c 1922; Leeds City Art Gallery

66

Marrows and Daisies. 36″ × 30″
Oil. Signed c 1922; Private Collection

Granaries, Ipswich. 12¼″ × 14½″
Watercolour and pencil. Signed and dated 1923; Ipswich Museums and Galleries

Chalk Pit in Chiltern Woods. 9⅜″ × 10⅝″
Watercolour and pencil. Signed and dated 1923; Private Collection

The Woodland Ride (Sunlight through trees). 9¼″ × 8¼″
Oil. Not signed c 1925; Buckinghamshire County Museum

The Grove. 22″ × 17¼″
Watercolour and pencil. Signed 1936; Private Collection

The Deserted Sheep-pen. 15" × 25¼"
Oil. Signed c 1930; Northampton Museums

72

The Mill Pond. 15½″ × 22″
Oil. Signed c 1936; Private Collection

The Black Barn, Bottemgoms Farm. 17″ × 21″
Watercolour. Signed, inscribed and dated 1948; Private Collection

China Clay Workings, St. Austell, Cornwall. 15½″ × 19½″
Watercolour. Signed and dated 1950; Private Collection

Disused Canal at Wormingford. 24″ × 30″
Oil. Signed c 1958; Towner Art Gallery, Eastbourne

Iris Kochii. 15¾″ × 12⅛″
Watercolour and ink. Signed and inscribed, c 1962; Private Collection

Frozen Ponds. 23¼″ × 29½″
Oil. Signed and dated 1959; Private Collection

Worms Head, Gower Peninsula. 15″ × 21″
Watercolour. Signed c 1963; Private Collection

Men Afield. 22¼ × 35¾″
Oil. Signed and dated 1964; Private Collection

The Garden in Winter. 25″ × 30″
Oil. Signed c 1964; Colchester Museum

Edale. 30″ × 36″
Oil. Signed c 1964; Private Collection

Campanula Canaryensis. 11½″ × 8¾″
Watercolour. Signed and inscribed c 1965; Private Collection

83

Campsis. 16⅝″ × 9½″
Watercolour. Signed; Private Collection

Sunflowers in a Jam Jar. 16⅝″ × 9½″
Watercolour and pencil. Signed and inscribed 1968; Private Collection

85

Autumn Crocus (Crocus Bornmulleri). 11¼″ × 8½″
Watercolour and pencil. Signed 1968; Private Collection

86

Staverton Thicks. 20″ × 30″
Oil. Signed, not dated; Private Collection

Ice and Snow
Oil. Signed and dated 1969; Private Collection

Landscape on Skye. 11¼″ × 8¾″
Watercolour and pencil. Signed c 1974; Private Collection

Buildings in Gloucestershire. 12¼″ × 16¼″
Pencil and wash. Signed and dated 1920; Private Collection

Bristol Docks. 12″ × 15″
Watercolour. Signed c 1925; Private Collection

Threshing in a farmyard near Princes Risborough. 8¾″ × 11⅝″
Pencil. Not signed c 1928; Buckinghamshire County Museum

Pulteney Bridge, Bath. 15¼" × 20¼"
Sepia wash. Not signed c 1925; Private Collection

Woods in Winter. 10¾″ × 14¾″
Watercolour and ink. Signed c 1926, Whitworth Art Gallery, Manchester

Bledlow Ridge. 11″ × 15″
Oil sketch. Not signed c 1928; Private Collection

The Edge of the Plain 20″ × 24″
Oil. Signed c 1928; Fitzwilliam Museum, Cambridge

A Window in Bucks (Snow Scene, Meadle). 36″ × 30″
Oil. Signed and dated 1928; Private Collection

Wormingford Mill. 15¼" × 20¼"
Pencil. Signed and dated 1929; Chelmsford Art Gallery

Disused Gravel Pit. 17¾″ × 24¼″
Watercolour and pencil. Signed c 1935; Walker Art Gallery, Liverpool

Winter Afternoon. 15¾″ × 23¼″
Watercolour and ink. Signed c 1950; Birmingham Museum and Art Gallery

Incoming Tide, Overstrand. 15¾″ × 20¾″
Watercolour. Signed c 1955; Walker Art Gallery, Liverpool

Rock Faces. 10″ × 14″
Watercolour and pencil. Signed c 1960; Private Collection

Dunwich Ruins. 11″ × 9″
Watercolour and pencil. Signed c 1955; Private Collection

The Quiraing, Skye: Sunset on a Loch. 17″ × 24″
Oil. Signed and dated 1959; Private Collection

Pheasants in the Snow. 17″ × 22″
Watercolour. Signed and dated 1968; Private Collection

Landscape near Boxted. 8¼″ × 11¼″
Watercolour and pencil. Signed, not dated

Cliffs at Covehithe. 15″ × 18″
Watercolour. Signed, dated 1970; Chelmsford Art Gallery

107

Norfolk Chalkpit. 13¾″ × 17½″
Pencil and wash. Signed c 1970; Private Collection

House-leek and Flints. 10¼″ × 8⅜″
Ink and watercolour. Signed and inscribed c 1950; Private Collection

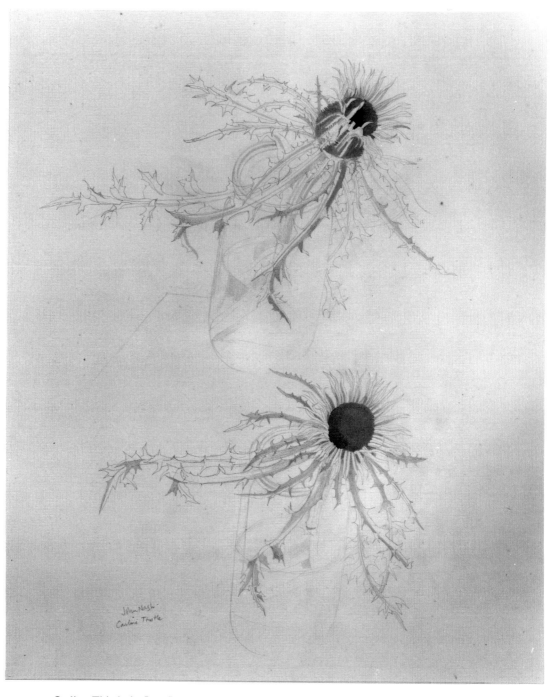

Carline Thistle in Jam Jar. 15⅞″ × 13¼″
Pencil and watercolour. Signed and inscribed c 1960; Buckinghamshire County Museum

Comic Drawing of Father Christmas Fishing. 5⅝″ × 6¼″
Biro. Signed c 1970; Buckinghamshire County Museum

Bibliography

John Nash, The Fleuron, 1925 (Preface by Sidney Schiff)

Dr. John Rothenstein, 'John Nash', *Picture Post*, 1 April 1939. Great British Masters Series 1927

Poet and Painter, being the correspondence between Gordon Bottomley and Paul Nash 1910–1946, edited by Claude Colleer Abbott and Anthony Bertram, Oxford, 1955

Paul Nash, *Outline: an autobiography and other writings*, Faber, 1949

Sir John Rothenstein, *Modern British Painters 2: Lewis to Moore*, Eyre and Spottiswoode, 1956

John Nash CBE, RA: Catalogue for an exhibition of paintings and drawings by John Nash with an introduction by Frederick Gore ARA, Royal Academy of Arts, 1967

William Feaver, 'A Sense of Place', *Sunday Times* Colour Supplement, 31 August 1975

John Lewis (with a foreword by Wilfred Blunt), *John Nash: The painter as illustrator*, Pendomer Press, 1978

Sir John Rothenstein, *John Nash*, MacDonald and Co., 1983

Clare Colvin, *John Nash: Book Designs*, The Minories, 1985

Jeremy Greenwood, *Wood Engravings by John Nash*, The Wood Lea Press, 1987

Claughton Pellew, Introduction by John Nash and Biographical Note by Anne Stevens, Fleece Press, 1987

Christopher Neve, *Unquiet Landscape*, Faber and Faber, 1990

Ronald Blythe, *John Nash at Wormingford*, Aldgate Press, 1991

Index of titles